SPORTS RECORDS
TO MAKE YOU CHEER!

KENNY ABDO

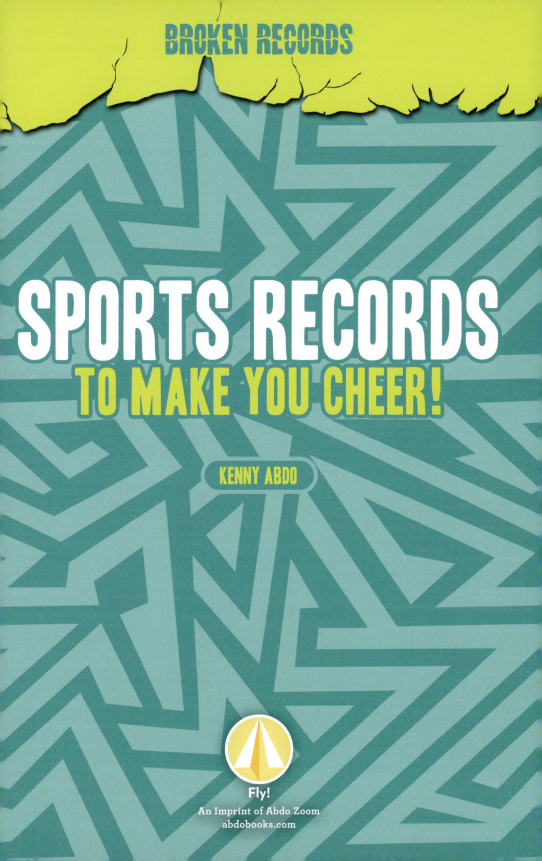

Fly!
An Imprint of Abdo Zoom
abdobooks.com

abdobooks.com

Published by Abdo Zoom, a division of ABDO, P.O. Box 398166, Minneapolis, Minnesota 55439. Copyright © 2024 by Abdo Consulting Group, Inc. International copyrights reserved in all countries. No part of this book may be reproduced in any form without written permission from the publisher. Fly!™ is a trademark and logo of Abdo Zoom.

Printed in the United States of America, North Mankato, Minnesota.
052023
092023

THIS BOOK CONTAINS RECYCLED MATERIALS

Photo Credits: Alamy, AP Images, Getty Images, Shutterstock
Production Contributors: Kenny Abdo, Jennie Forsberg, Grace Hansen
Design Contributors: Candice Keimig, Neil Klinepier, Laura Graphenteen

Library of Congress Control Number: 2022946922

Publisher's Cataloging-in-Publication Data

Names: Abdo, Kenny, author.
Title: Sports records to make you cheer! / by Kenny Abdo
Description: Minneapolis, Minnesota : Abdo Zoom, 2024 | Series: Broken records |
    Includes online resources and index.
Identifiers: ISBN 9781098281403 (lib. bdg.) | ISBN 9781098282103 (ebook) |
    ISBN 9781098282455 (Read-to-me ebook)
Subjects: LCSH: Records--Juvenile literature. | History--Juvenile literature. |
    Sports records--Juvenile literature.
Classification: DDC 032.02--dc23

TABLE OF CONTENTS

SPORTS RECORDS

Professional athletes have always wowed audiences with their skills. But when they break world records, it's a whole new ball game!

From incredible running speeds to unbreakable **hitting streaks**, these sports records will get crowds cheering!

don 2012

BROKEN RECORDS

New York Yankees center fielder Joe DiMaggio had a great season in 1941. He recorded at least one hit in 56 straight games.

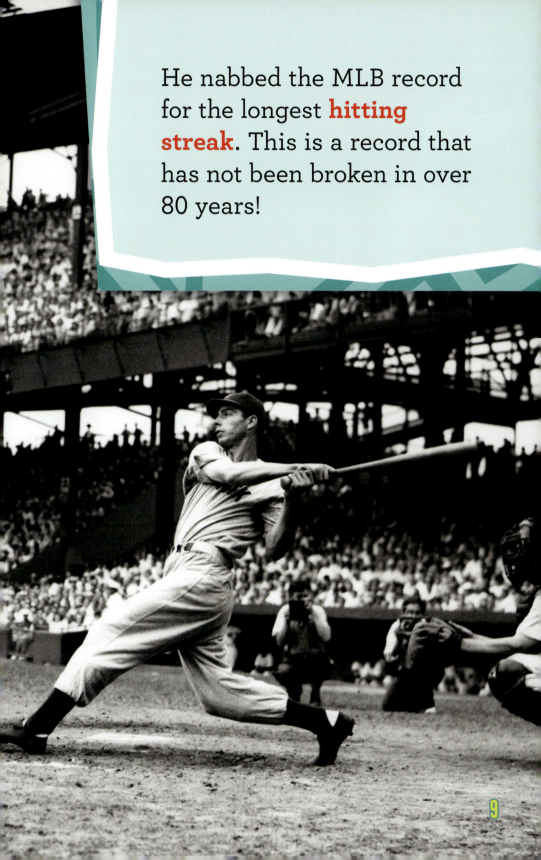

He nabbed the MLB record for the longest **hitting streak**. This is a record that has not been broken in over 80 years!

Nadia Comăneci made history at the 1976 Montreal **Olympics**. The 14-year-old Romanian gymnast was the first to be awarded a perfect 10 score. Comăneci also earned the **Guinness World Record** for being the first!

Runner Usain Bolt shocked the world at the 2009 Berlin World Athletics **Championship**. He broke the record for fastest time running the 100-meter dash. Reaching 28 mph (44.7 km/h) in just 9.58 seconds, he blew past the competition!

Max Verstappen became the youngest driver to win a Formula One World **Championship**. He reached first place at the 2016 Spanish Grand Prix. Verstappen was only 18 years old!

Serena Williams won her first **Grand Slam** singles **title** in 1999. She nabbed her 23rd at the 2017 Australian Open. Williams owns the record for longest span of Grand Slam singles titles, along with many other **Guinness World Records**!

In 2023, Tottenham Hotspur **striker** Harry Kane entered the history books. He scored his 267th goal for the team. Kane became the player to score the most career goals for a single club in the **English Premier League**!

FOR THE RECORD

Athletes continue to inspire their fans by being the best at what they do. And sometimes, they knock world records out of the park!

EIKO

WORLD RECORD

0mH

AUGHLIN

USA

50.6

GLOSSARY

championship – an event held to find a first-place winner.

English Premier League – the professional soccer organization that includes the top teams in England and Wales.

Grand Slam – winning all four major championships in the same calendar year.

Guinness World Record – an award given to those who have broken a record never achieved before.

hitting streak – in baseball, the consecutive number of official games in which a player gets at least one base hit.

Olympic Games – the biggest international athletic event held as separate winter and summer competitions every four years in a different city.

striker – in soccer, the player who plays closest to the opponent's goal.

title – a first-place position in a contest.

ONLINE RESOURCES

To learn more about sports records, please visit **abdobooklinks.com** or scan this QR code. These links are routinely monitored and updated to provide the most current information available.

INDEX